Editorial Manager
Karen J. Goldfluss, M.S. Ed.

Editor-in-Chief
Sharon Coan, M.S. Ed.

Cover Artist
Jessica Orlando

Creative Director
Elayne Roberts

Art Coordinator
Denice Adorno

Product Manager
Phil Garcia

Imaging
James Edward Grace

Publishers
Rachelle Cracchiolo, M.S. Ed.
Mary Dupuy Smith, M.S. Ed.

How Multiply

Grades 3–4

Author

Robert Smith

Teacher Created Materials, Inc.
6421 Industry Way
Westminster, CA 92683
www.teachercreated.com
ISBN-1-57690-484-9
©2000 Teacher Created Materials, Inc.
Reprinted, 2004
Made in U.S.A.

Table of Contents

A Note to Teachers and Parents

Welcome to the "How to" math series! You have chosen one of over two dozen books designed to give your children the information and practice they need to acquire important concepts in specific areas of math. The goal of the "How to" math books is to give children an extra boost as they work toward mastery of the math skills established by the National Council of Teachers of Mathematics (NCTM) and outlined in grade level scope and sequence guidelines.

The design of this book is intended to allow it to be used by teachers or parents for a variety of purposes and needs. Each of the units contains one or more "How to" pages and two or more practice pages. The "How to" section of each unit precedes the practice pages and provides needed information such as a concept or math rule review, important terms and formulas to remember, or step-by-step guidelines necessary for using the practice pages. While most "How to" pages are written for direct use by the children, in some lower grade level books these pages are presented as instructional pages or direct lessons to be used by a teacher or parent prior to introducing the practice pages.

About This Book

How to Multiply: Grades 3– 4 presents a comprehensive overview of multiplication of whole numbers with clear, simple, readable instruction pages for each unit. It can, therefore, be used to introduce and teach multiplication to children with little or no background in the concepts.

The units in this book can be used in whole-class instruction with the teacher or by a parent assisting his or her child through the book. This book also lends itself to use by a small group doing remedial or review work on multiplication or by individuals and small groups in earlier grades engaged in enrichment or advanced work. A teacher may want to have two tracks within his or her class with one moving at a faster pace and the other at a gradual pace appropriate to the ability or background of the students. This book can also be used in a learning center with materials specified for each unit of instruction.

Teachers and parents working with children who are new to the concept or who have not mastered their basic facts should have the children use the chart provided in Unit 1 until the tables are learned through time and use. Students should also be allowed to use the calculator to check the accuracy of their work. This reduces the need for correction and allows the material to be self-corrected if desired.

Where possible, integrate the opposite operation and help children recognize that multiplication and division are inverse operations closely related in both concept and process.

If children have difficulty on a specific concept or unit within this book, review the material and allow them to redo the troublesome pages. Since concept development is sequential, it is not advisable to skip much of the material in this book. It is preferable that children find the work easy and gradually advance to the more difficult concepts.

Encourage children to use manipulatives to reinforce the concepts. Using pennies, corn kernels, pinto beans, plastic counters, and similar materials with simple multiplication problems enhances a child's confidence and grasp of the concepts.

How to Multiply: Grades 3– 4 highlights the use of various mental math and estimation activities and emphasizes the development of proficiency in the use of the basic multiplication facts and the processes for doing multiplication. It provides a wide variety of instructional models and explanations for the gradual and thorough development of multiplication concepts and processes. It also provides specific multiplication techniques for dealing with word applications. Calculators are integrated within the text when appropriate.

The units in this book are designed to match the suggestions of the National Council of the Teachers of Mathematics (NCTM). They strongly support the learning of multiplication and other processes in the context of problem solving and real world applications. Use every opportunity to have students apply these new skills in classroom situations and at home. This will reinforce the value of the skill as well as the process. This book matches a number of NCTM standards including these main topics and specific features:

Problem Solving

This book offers many opportunities to apply basic multiplication computational skills in word problem formats and with real life applications. Children will also develop facility and confidence in their computational ability and in their ability to apply mathematics meaningfully.

Connections

The problems in this workbook help students see how mathematical ideas are related, especially in terms of multiplication and its inverse operation, division. Children also draw connections between multiplication and addition and recognize the use and application of multiplication in mathematics and in their daily lives.

Number and Operation

The material in this workbook conforms well to this standard which emphasizes the learning of numbers and number facts. The activities emphasize the use of numbers in concrete, physical ways by using manipulatives and by developing the relationship between numbers, the relationship of operations. Counting, grouping, and place value as they relate to multiplication are reinforced.

Other Standards

Children use **estimation** to determine the reasonableness of an answer. They explore ways to use estimation with various multiplication computations and word problems.

Children also develop competency in applying basic facts and performing mental **computations**.

Facts to Know

- Multiplication is just a rapid way to add the same number several times. For example, 7 + 7 + 7 + 7 + 7 is the same as 5 times 7 or 35.

$$
\begin{array}{r}
7 \\
7 \\
7 \\
7 \\
+\,7 \\
\hline
35
\end{array}
$$

Adding five 7's is the same as multiplying 7 times 5.

7 x 5 = 35

- The order of the numbers does not change the fact. For example, 7 x 5 = 35 and 5 x 7 = 35.

The multiplication chart shown here can be used to find any basic multiplication fact until you have learned them all.

One of the best ways to learn the facts is to practice using the chart.

Columns

Rows	1	2	3	4	5	6	7	8	9	10	11	12
1	1	2	3	4	5	6	7	8	9	10	11	12
2	2	4	6	8	10	12	14	16	18	20	22	24
3	3	6	9	12	15	18	21	24	27	30	33	36
4	4	8	12	16	20	24	28	32	36	40	44	48
5	5	10	15	20	25	30	35	40	45	50	55	60
6	6	12	18	24	30	36	42	48	54	60	66	72
7	7	14	21	28	35	42	49	56	63	70	77	84
8	8	16	24	32	40	48	56	64	72	80	88	96
9	9	18	27	36	45	54	63	72	81	90	99	108
10	10	20	30	40	50	60	70	80	90	100	110	120
11	11	22	33	44	55	66	77	88	99	110	121	132
12	12	24	36	48	60	72	84	96	108	120	132	144

Read down for the *columns*
Read across for the *rows*.

Note: To find 4 times 8, run one finger down the 4 column and a finger on the other hand across the 8 row until they meet. The answer is the number 32 where the row and column intersect (meet).

$$4 \quad + \quad 4 \quad + \quad 4 \quad + \quad 4 \quad + \quad 4$$

$$= 5 \times 4$$

$$5 \times 4 = 20$$

Directions: Use the multiplication chart on page 5 to help you find the answers to these problems. Add the numbers to check your answers.

1.   8
        8
        8
    + 8

2. $4 \times 8 = \underline{\hphantom{00}}$

3.   6
        6
        6
        6
    + 6

4. $5 \times 6 = \underline{\hphantom{00}}$

5.   7
        7
    + 7

6. $3 \times 7 = \underline{\hphantom{00}}$

7.   9
        9
        9
        9
    + 9

8. $9 \times 5 = \underline{\hphantom{00}}$

9.   12
      12
      12
      12
      12
  + 12

10. $12 \times 6 = \underline{\hphantom{00}}$

11. 10
       10
       10
   + 10

12. $4 \times 10 = \underline{\hphantom{00}}$

13. $7 \times 6 = \underline{\hphantom{00}}$

14. $8 \times 4 = \underline{\hphantom{00}}$

15. $7 \times 9 = \underline{\hphantom{00}}$

16.   9
    x 8

17. 12
   x 8

18. 7
   x 5

19. $8 \times 8 = \underline{\hphantom{00}}$

20. $9 \times 8 = \underline{\hphantom{00}}$

21. $4 \times 6 = \underline{\hphantom{00}}$

22. $11 \times 11 = \underline{\hphantom{00}}$

23. $8 \times 7 = \underline{\hphantom{00}}$

24. $9 \times 7 = \underline{\hphantom{00}}$

There are 4 tires on each car.
There are 6 cars.

| How many tires are there? | 4 x 6 = _____ |

Directions: Use the multiplication chart on page 5 to help you find the answers to these problems.

1. 6 x 9 = ____   **2.** 7 x 7 = ____   **3.** 5 x 8 = ____   **4.** 9 x 4 = ____

5. 9 x 8 = ____   **6.** 8 x 8 = ____   **7.** 7   **8.** 9
                                                    x 8   x 6

9. 11   **10.** 4   **11.** 6   **12.** 12   **13.** 11
     x 5   x 6   x 6   x 8   x 9

14. 8   **15.** 8   **16.** 4 x 3 = ____   **17.** 3 x 4 = ____   **18.** 9 x 12 = ____
     x 7   x 3

19. 12 x 9 = ____   **20.** 11 x 10 = ____   **21.** 10 x 11 = ____   **22.** 5 x 7 = ____

23. 7 x 5 = ____   **24.** 8 x 6 = ____   **25.** 6   **26.** 7
                                                    x 8   x 9

27. 9   **28.** 7   **29.** 9   **30.** 12   **31.** 6   **32.** 5   **33.** 10
     x 7   x 7   x 9   x 12   x 6   x 5   x 10

What are the missing numbers?

Rows	Columns											
	1	2	3	4	5	6	7	8	9	10	11	12
1	1	2	3	4	5	6	7	8	9	10	11	12
2	2	4	6	8	10	12	14	16	18	20	22	24
3	3	6	9	12	15	18	21	24	27	30	33	36

(2, 4, 6, 8, 10, 12, 14, 16, _____, _____, _____, _____)

Directions: Use the <u>rows</u> on the multiplication chart on page 5 to help you find the missing numbers.

1. (3, 6, 9, 12, 15, 18, _____, _____, _____, _____ , 33, 36)

2. (5, 10, 15, 20, 25, _____, _____, _____, _____, _____, _____, _____)

3. (4, 8, 12, 16, _____, _____, _____, _____, _____, _____, _____, _____)

4. (9, 18 , 27, 36, _____, _____, _____, _____, _____, _____, _____, _____)

5. (10, 20, 30, 40, _____, _____, _____, _____, _____, _____, _____, _____)

6. (7, 14, 21, 28, _____, _____, _____, _____, _____, _____, _____, _____)

7. (2, 4, 6, 8, _____, _____, _____, _____, _____, _____, _____, _____)

8. (8, 16, 24, _____, _____, _____, _____, _____, _____, _____, _____)

9. (6, 12, 18, 24, _____, _____, _____, _____, _____, _____, _____, _____)

10. (12, 24, 36, 48, 60, _____, _____, _____, _____, _____, _____, _____)

Directions: Use the chart on page 5 to answer these questions.

11. Which row in the chart has exactly the same numbers as in problem one above? _____

12. Which row in the chart has exactly the same numbers as in problem 10 above? _____

13. Draw a diagonal line through your chart which shows each number multiplied by itself.

14. How much does each number in the ones row add up to? _____

15. Which column has a zero in every number? _____

Facts to Know

- A *factor* is a number which divides exactly into another number.
- When two or more factors are multiplied, they form a *product.*

Sample 1

4 x 7 = 28

factor   factor   product

The numbers 4 and 7 are factors of the product 28.

- A factor tree is a chart which illustrates the prime factors of a number.

- A *prime factor* is a number that can only be the product of 1 and itself.

Sample 2

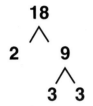

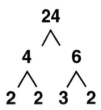

The prime factors of 18 are 2 and 3. (2 x 3 x 3 = 18)

The prime factors of 24 are 2 and 3. (2 x 2 x 2 x 3 = 24)

- You can use the chart on page 5 to find missing factors.

Sample 3

3 x _____ = 24

1. Run a finger down the column of 3's until you reach 24.

2. Run a finger left across the row from 24 until you reach the 8.

3. Therefore 3 x 8 = 24. The missing factor is 8.

	Columns											
Rows	**1**	**2**	**3**	**4**	**5**	**6**	**7**	**8**	**9**	**10**	**11**	**12**
1	1	2	3	4	5	6	7	8	9	10	11	12
2	2	4	6	8	10	12	14	16	18	20	22	24
3	3	6	9	12	15	18	21	24	27	30	33	36

How many groups of 5 pennies do you see? How many pennies are in the picture altogether?

The numbers 5 and 6 are factors of the product 30.

Directions: Use pennies to compute these answers.

1. 7 groups of 3 pennies = _____ pennies

2. 5 groups of 4 pennies = _____ pennies

3. 6 groups of 7 pennies = _____ pennies

4. 3 groups of 9 pennies = _____ pennies

5. 8 groups of 5 pennies = _____ pennies

6. 4 groups of 12 pennies = _____ pennies

7. 5 groups of 9 pennies = _____ pennies

8. 6 groups of 6 pennies = _____ pennies

Directions: Use pennies to compute these answers.

9. 8 groups of 3 = _____

10. 4 groups of 9 = _____

11. 7 groups of 6 = _____

12. 6 groups of 9 = _____

13. 9 groups of 11 = _____

14. 8 groups of 12 = _____

15. 8 groups of 10 = _____

16. 5 groups of 8 = _____

17. 3 groups of 3 = _____

18. 9 groups of 9 = _____

19. 8 groups of 6 = _____

20. 9 groups of 8 = _____

21. 3 groups of 11 = _____

22. 11 groups of 9 = _____

23. 7 groups of 7 = _____

24. 7 groups of 9 = _____

25. 8 groups of 11 = _____

26. 7 groups of 11 = _____

27. 6 groups of 3 = _____

28. 6 groups of 11 = _____

29. 11 groups of 3 = _____

30. 10 groups of 9 = _____

These are factor trees. A factor tree is used to determine the prime factors of a number. (**Reminder:** A prime factor is a number that can only be the product of one and itself.)

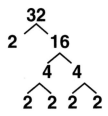

The prime factors of 14 are 2 and 7. (2 x 7 = 14)

The prime factors of 20 are 5 and 2. (5 x 2 x 2 = 20)

The prime factor of 32 is 2. (2 x 2 x 2 x 2 x 2 = 32)

Factor trees can be made using several patterns to reach the prime numbers. Whichever tree pattern you choose, you will eventually reach the same prime numbers.

Directions: Use factor trees to determine the prime factors of these numbers. The first two are started for you.

1.   30

2.   28

3.   42

4.   44

5.   50

6.   66

7.   77

8.   63

9.   15

10.   18

11.   22

12.   36

13.   8

14.   64

15.   25

16.   125

2 ► Practice ••• Finding Missing Factors in Equations

Directions: Use the chart on page 5 to help you find the missing factors.

1. 9 x _____ = 72

2. 8 x _____ = 64

3. 6 x _____ = 54

4. 8 x _____ = 40

5. 7 x _____ = 42

6. 6 x _____ = 30

7. 9 x _____ = 27

8. 9 x _____ = 81

9. 7 x _____ = 63

10. 7 x _____ = 49

11. 6 x _____ = 54

12. 5 x _____ = 60

13. _____ x 5 = 40

14. _____ x 3 = 27

15. _____ x 4 = 36

16. _____ x 7 = 56

17. _____ x 6 = 48

18. _____ x 10 = 40

19. _____ x 8 = 72

20. _____ x 9 = 45

21. _____ x 11 = 121

22. _____ x 4 = 44

23. _____ x 6 = 12

24. _____ x 12 = 60

Directions: Solve the equations. (The factor in both blanks is the same.)

25. _____ x _____ = 64

26. _____ x _____ = 100

27. _____ x _____ = 36

28. _____ x _____ = 81

29. _____ x _____ = 49

30. _____ x _____ = 121

Facts to Know

The following samples help you "picture" multiplication by one-digit multipliers.

Sample A

Each egg carton holds 12 eggs.

You could add 12 + 12 + 12 to calculate the number of eggs.

Multiplication is quicker. Just multiply 3 times 12.

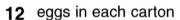

    12 eggs in each carton
  x 3 cartons
  ─────────
    36 eggs all together

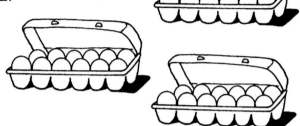

Sample B

You can multiply larger numbers this way:
You have 5 bags of marbles. Each bag holds 25 marbles.

      25
  x   5
  ─────────
      25 (5 times 5 equals 25)
     100 (5 times 20 equals 100)
     125 (add 25 and 100)

Sample C

Another way to multiply large numbers is by regrouping.

Step by Step

1. Multiply 5 (ones) times 5 (ones) to equal 25 (2 tens and 5 ones).

2. Write the 5 in the ones place and place the 2 (tens) above the tens place.

3. Multiply 5 (ones) times 2 (tens) to equal 10 (tens). Add the number carried to get the 12 (tens).

4. The complete answer is 125 (12 tens and 5 ones).

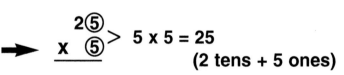

$$5 \times 5 = 25$$
(2 tens + 5 ones)

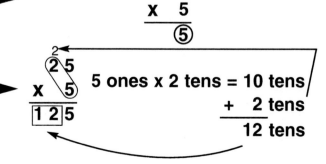

5 ones x 2 tens = 10 tens
+   2 tens
─────────────
12 tens

Directions: Use the multiplication chart on page 5 and the information on page 13 to help you complete this page.

```
  12
x  3
────
  36
```

1. 32
    x 4

2. 43
    x 3

3. 14
    x 2

4. 33
    x 3

5. 23
    x 2

6. 12
    x 4

7. 43
    x 2

8. 67
    x 1

9. 34
    x 2

10. 73
    x 2

11. 31
    x 4

12. 23
    x 3

Directions: Rewrite these problems in the ladder form as shown below and multiply.

ladder form

```
13 x 3 =      13
            x  3
            ────
              39
```

13. 5 x 41 = ____

14. 4 x 22 = ____

15. 2 x 44 = ____

16. 2 x 93 = ____

17. 2 x 24 = ____

18. 9 x 11 = ____

Directions: Complete the computations below. Use the information on page 13 and the multiplication chart on page 5 if you need help.

Step by Step

	hundreds	tens	ones
		4	
		3	5
x			9
	3	1	5

1. Multiply 9 (ones) times 5 (ones) to equal 45 (4 tens and 5 ones).
2. Write the 5 below the line (in the ones place) and regroup by carrying the 4 tens above the tens column.
3. Multiply 9 (ones) times 3 (tens) to equal 27 tens.
4. Add the regrouped 4 tens to the 27 tens to equal 31 tens.
5. Write the 1 (ten) in the tens place and the 3 (hundreds) in the hundreds place.
6. The final answer is 315.

1. 39
   x 3

2. 63
   x 7

3. 22
   x 7

4. 37
   x 4

5. 48
   x 6

6. 66
   x 5

7. 25
   x 7

8. 38
   x 6

9. 42
   x 9

10. 18
    x 6

11. 47
    x 5

12. 88
    x 5

Directions: Rewrite these problems in the ladder form and multiply.

$$8 \times 43 = \underline{\hspace{1cm}}$$

$$\begin{array}{r} \overset{2}{43} \\ \times\ 8 \\ \hline 344 \end{array} \longleftarrow \text{ladder form}$$

13. 4 x 63 = _____

14. 5 x 65 = _____

15. 9 x 84 = _____

16. 7 x 75 = _____

17. 9 x 54 = _____

18. 9 x 99 = _____

19. 7 x 49 = _____

20. 8 x 79 = _____

Step by Step

	hundreds	tens	ones
	1	2	
	1	**3**	**5**
x			**5**
	6	**7**	**5**

1. Multiply 5 ones times 5 ones to equal 25 (2 tens and 5 ones).
2. Write the 5 below the line (in the ones place) and regroup by carrying the 2 tens above the tens column.
3. Multiply 5 times 3 tens to get 15 tens. Add the regrouped 2 tens to the 15 tens to get 17 tens.
4. Place the 7 tens below the line and regroup by placing the 1 above the hundreds place.
5. Next, multiply 5 times 1 hundred to equal 5 hundred.
6. Add the regrouped 1 hundred to the 5 hundred to equal 6 hundred and place the 6 below the line in the hundreds place.
7. The answer is 675.

Directions: Complete the computations below. Use the example above and the chart on page 5 if you need help.

1. 369 x 3	**2.** 428 x 6	**3.** 123 x 5	**4.** 865 x 3
5. 927 x 4	**6.** 889 x 7	**7.** 664 x 5	**8.** 693 x 9
9. 739 x 6	**10.** 747 x 7	**11.** 999 x 9	**12.** 688 x 4

Directions: Rewrite these problems in the ladder form (as shown in problem 13) and multiply.

13.   7 x 785 = _____

785
x   7

14.   3 x 607 = _____

15.   7 x 897 = _____

16.   8 x 527 = _____

17.   8 x 493 = _____

18.   9 x 109 = _____

Facts to Know

You can use mental math to multiply by 10. With practice you can probably multiply these problems in your head as quickly as you can use a calculator!

- To multiply any number by 10, just add a zero to the number being multiplied.

   If you have 10 bags of candy and each bag has 32 candies, you would have 320 candies altogether.

Sample A

```
   32
x  10
  320
```
32 x 10 = 320

- To multiply any number by 100, just add two zeros to the number being multiplied.

   If you have 100 hundred bags and each bag has 45 marbles, you would have a total of 4500 marbles.

Sample B

```
    45
x  100
 4,500
```

1 ⃝00⃝ x 45 = 4,5 ⃝00⃝

- To multiply any number by 1000, just add three zeros to the number being multiplied.

Sample C

```
     3569
x    1000
3,569,000
```

1 ⃝000⃝ x 3569 = 3,569, ⃝000⃝

- Place commas in answers where needed. **85 x 1000 = 85,000**

Shortcut to Finding the Product When Factors Are Multiples of 10

When one or more of the numbers being multiplied are multiples of 10, follow these steps:

```
2,000,000
x  12,000
```

1. Multiply the parts of each factor that are not zeros. (2 x 12 = 24)

2. For each of the numbers being multiplied, find the number of zeros from left to right (before reaching a non-zero number) and add the same number of zeros to the product. (In this example, there are 9 zeros. The product should have 9 zeros.)

2,⃝000,000⃝ x 12,⃝000⃝ = 24,⃝000,000,000⃝

To multiply any number by 10, just add a 0 to the number being multiplied.

Each bag holds 13 peanuts. There are 10 bags. Altogether there are 130 peanuts.

Directions: Use the information on page 17 to compute these answers.

1. 14 x 10	**2.** 16 x 10	**3.** 45 x 10	**4.** 65 x 10
5. 19 x 10	**6.** 17 x 10	**7.** 22 x 10	**8.** 37 x 10
9. 38 x 10	**10.** 98 x 10	**11.** 76 x 10	**12.** 65 x 10

13. 68 x 10 = _____   **14.** 77 x 10 = _____   **15.** 73 x 10 = _____

16. 33 x 10 = _____   **17.** 35 x 10 = _____   **18.** 53 x 10 = _____

Directions: Compute these answers in your mind. Write the answer in the space provided.

19. 986 x 10	**20.** 872 x 10	**21.** 621 x 10	**22.** 765 x 10
23. 543 x 10	**24.** 9767 x 10	**25.** 7502 x 10	**26.** 1043 x 10

27. 8976 x 10 = _____   **28.** 6004 x 10 = _____

To multiply by 100, add two zeros to the number being multiplied.

$$\begin{array}{r} 52 \\ \times 100 \\ \hline 5,200 \end{array}$$

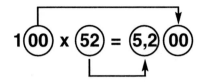

There are 52 playing cards in a regular deck of cards. In 100 decks of cards there are 5,200 cards.

Directions: Use the information on page 17 to help you compute these answers.

1. 7 x 100 = _____   2. 8 x 100 = _____   3. 4 x 100 = _____

4. 43 x 100 = _____   5. 32 x 100 = _____   6. 51 x 100 = _____

7. $\begin{array}{r} 54 \\ \times\ 100 \\ \hline \end{array}$ 8. $\begin{array}{r} 26 \\ \times\ 100 \\ \hline \end{array}$ 9. $\begin{array}{r} 62 \\ \times\ 100 \\ \hline \end{array}$ 10. $\begin{array}{r} 98 \\ \times\ 100 \\ \hline \end{array}$

11. $\begin{array}{r} 989 \\ \times\ 100 \\ \hline \end{array}$ 12. $\begin{array}{r} 447 \\ \times\ 100 \\ \hline \end{array}$ 13. $\begin{array}{r} 826 \\ \times\ 100 \\ \hline \end{array}$ 14. $\begin{array}{r} 73 \\ \times\ 100 \\ \hline \end{array}$

15. 659 x 100 _____   16. 749 x 100 = _____

17. $\begin{array}{r} 8974 \\ \times\ \ 100 \\ \hline \end{array}$ 18. $\begin{array}{r} 5,439 \\ \times\ \ 100 \\ \hline \end{array}$ 19. $\begin{array}{r} 5638 \\ \times\ \ 100 \\ \hline \end{array}$

20. 6,549 x 100 = _____   21. 8732 x 100 = _____

22. $\begin{array}{r} 22,202 \\ \times\ \ 100 \\ \hline \end{array}$ 23. $\begin{array}{r} 65,804 \\ \times\ \ 100 \\ \hline \end{array}$ 24. $\begin{array}{r} 97,527 \\ \times\ \ 100 \\ \hline \end{array}$

25. 765,905 x 100 = _____

To multiply by 1000, add three zeros to the number being multiplied.

If you have 9 bags of marbles and each bag has 1000 marbles in it, there are 9000 marbles altogether.

9 x 1000 = 9,000

Directions: Use the information on page 17 to help you compute these answers.

1. 5 x 1000 = _____   **2.** 7 x 1000 = _____   **3.** 3 x 1000 = _____

4. 65 x 1000 = _____   **5.** 23 x 1000 = _____   **6.** 14 x 1000 = _____

7. 67 x 1000	**8.** 21 x 1000	**9.** 99 x 1000	**10.** 76 x 1000
11. 654 x 1000	**12.** 785 x 1000	**13.** 806 x 1000	**14.** 117 x 1000

```
  3467
x 1000
3,467,000
```

4594 x 1000 = 4,594,000

Directions: Use the sample above to help you solve these problems.

15. 3943 x 1000	**16.** 4607 x 1000	**17.** 1840 x 1000
18. 5006 x 1000	**19.** 9478 x 1000	**20.** 2001 x 1000

21. 7958 x 1000 = _____   **22.** 2980 x 1000 = _____

23. 43767 x 1000 = _____   **24.** 99,759 x 1000 = _____

25. 876,423 x 1000 = _____   **26.** 756,000 x 1000 = _____

20

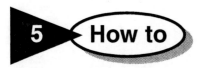
Facts to Know

- A *multiple* of any number is the product of that number and another number. For example, 15 is a multiple of 5, since 5 times another number (3) equals 15. Other multiples of 5 are 20, 25, 30, 35, and so on. Some multiples of 10 are 20, 30, 40, 50, and 100.

- To multiply a number by a multiple of 10, follow the steps in the sample below.

Sample A

1. Arrange the numbers in the ladder format.

$$\begin{array}{r} 45 \\ \times\ 20 \\ \hline \end{array}$$

45 x 20 =

2. Drop the zero as an "automatic zero" or placeholder.

$$\begin{array}{r} 45 \\ \times\ 2\textcircled{0} \\ \hline 0 \end{array}$$ ◄ (automatic zero)

3. Multiply the non-zero numbers (2 and 45).

$$\begin{array}{r} \boxed{45} \\ \times\ \boxed{2}0 \\ \hline \textcircled{90}\,0 \end{array}$$

- To multiply a number by a multiple of 100 (200, 300, or 500, for example), follow the same steps as above.

Sample B

1. Arrange the numbers in the ladder format.

$$\begin{array}{r} 325 \\ \times\ 300 \\ \hline \end{array}$$

325 x 300 =

2. Drop both zeros as "automatic zeros" or placeholders.

$$\begin{array}{r} 325 \\ \times\ 3\textcircled{00} \\ \hline 00 \end{array}$$ ◄ (automatic zeros)

3. Multiply the non-zero numbers (3 and 325).

$$\begin{array}{r} \boxed{325} \\ \times\ \boxed{3}00 \\ \hline \textcircled{97,5}00 \end{array}$$

Each sheet of stickers holds 12 star stickers. There are 20 sheets in a package. How many star stickers are there in the package?

$$\begin{array}{r} 12 \\ \times\ 20 \\ \hline 240 \end{array}$$

Directions: Use the chart on page 5 and the information on page 21 to help you complete these problems.

1.
$$\begin{array}{r} 12 \\ \times\ 30 \\ \hline \end{array}$$

2.
$$\begin{array}{r} 14 \\ \times\ 20 \\ \hline \end{array}$$

3.
$$\begin{array}{r} 13 \\ \times\ 30 \\ \hline \end{array}$$

4.
$$\begin{array}{r} 19 \\ \times\ 40 \\ \hline \end{array}$$

5.
$$\begin{array}{r} 18 \\ \times\ 20 \\ \hline \end{array}$$

6.
$$\begin{array}{r} 16 \\ \times\ 50 \\ \hline \end{array}$$

7.
$$\begin{array}{r} 12 \\ \times\ 90 \\ \hline \end{array}$$

8.
$$\begin{array}{r} 21 \\ \times\ 30 \\ \hline \end{array}$$

9.
$$\begin{array}{r} 28 \\ \times\ 20 \\ \hline \end{array}$$

10.
$$\begin{array}{r} 81 \\ \times\ 30 \\ \hline \end{array}$$

11.
$$\begin{array}{r} 27 \\ \times\ 40 \\ \hline \end{array}$$

12.
$$\begin{array}{r} 25 \\ \times\ 50 \\ \hline \end{array}$$

13.
$$\begin{array}{r} 19 \\ \times\ 30 \\ \hline \end{array}$$

14.
$$\begin{array}{r} 22 \\ \times\ 70 \\ \hline \end{array}$$

15.
$$\begin{array}{r} 89 \\ \times\ 90 \\ \hline \end{array}$$

16.
$$\begin{array}{r} 33 \\ \times\ 70 \\ \hline \end{array}$$

17.
$$\begin{array}{r} 99 \\ \times\ 40 \\ \hline \end{array}$$

18.
$$\begin{array}{r} 65 \\ \times\ 90 \\ \hline \end{array}$$

19.
$$\begin{array}{r} 17 \\ \times\ 20 \\ \hline \end{array}$$

20.
$$\begin{array}{r} 41 \\ \times\ 90 \\ \hline \end{array}$$

Directions: Use the chart on page 5 and the information on page 21 to help you complete these problems. Rewrite the problems in the ladder form. The first one is rewritten for you.

21. 30 x 38 = _____

$$\begin{array}{r} 38 \\ \times\ 30 \\ \hline \end{array}$$

22. 20 x 47 = _____

23. 40 x 43 = _____

24. 80 x 87 = _____

25. 20 x 67 = _____

26. 60 x 39 = _____

$$3 \times 5 = 15$$

```
  300
x  50
-------
15,000
```

$$300 \times 50 = 15,\boxed{000}$$

There are 3 zeros.

Directions: Use the information on page 21 and review the shortcut information on page 17 to help you find these answers.

1. 400 x 30	2. 500 x 90	3. 900 x 60	4. 700 x 40
5. 800 x 80	6. 500 x 70	7. 200 x 70	8. 400 x 60
9. 700 x 60	10. 100 x 90	11. 700 x 30	12. 600 x 70

Directions: Solve these problems. Check your answers carefully. (*Remember: Any number multiplied by zero is zero.*)

13. 304 x 20	14. 907 x 80	15. 902 x 70	16. 509 x 40
17. 209 x 50	18. 709 x 40	19. 603 x 60	20. 809 x 30

Directions: Use the information on page 21 to help you find these answers.

21. 221 x 20	22. 632 x 30	23. 741 x 70	24. 515 x 30
25. 873 x 30	26. 823 x 40	27. 472 x 40	28. 863 x 60

Step by Step

1. Write the problem vertically as shown.
2. Drop two "automatic" zeros into the product.
3. Multiply 3 x 453.
4. Remember to regroup.

ladder form

$$453$$
$$x\ 300$$
$$135,900 \quad 3 \times 453 = 1359$$

Directions: Use the information on page 21 to solve these problems.

1. 232 x 200	2. 384 x 300	3. 733 x 500	4. 673 x 400
5. 238 x 700	6. 876 x 300	7. 322 x 900	8. 721 x 500
9. 461 x 400	10. 984 x 200	11. 783 x 600	12. 877 x 700
13. 638 x 400	14. 954 x 300	15. 244 x 900	16. 155 x 600

Directions: Use the information on page 21 and the chart on page 5 to complete these problems. Rewrite the problems in the ladder form. The first two problems are rewritten for you.

17. 200 x 763 = _____

763
x 200

18. 300 x 644 = _____

644
x 300

19. 500 x 956 = _____

20. 300 x 341 = _____

21. 500 x 632 = _____

22. 500 x 934 = _____

23. 555 x 300 = _____

24. 234 x 500 = _____

25. 929 x 600 = _____

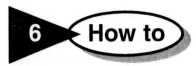

Facts to Know

To multiply 45 x 23, follow this sample.

Step by Step

1. Write the problem in ladder form.

$$\begin{array}{r} 23 \\ \times\ 45 \\ \hline \end{array}$$

2. Multiply 5 ones times 23.

3. Remember to regroup and add the 1 above the tens place. (Note: Erase or cross out the regrouped 1 when you have finished adding it.) The answer is 115. This is called a *partial product* since it represents only part of the product.

$$\begin{array}{r} \overset{1}{23} \\ \times\ 45 \\ \hline 115 \end{array}$$ partial product

4. Write the automatic zero (placeholder) in the ones place, below the 5. You have already multiplied the ones place number (5). The zero is a reminder that you are now multiplying by the tens place digit (4).

$$\begin{array}{r} \overset{1}{23} \\ \times\ 45 \\ \hline 115 \\ 0 \end{array}$$ (23 x 5)   automatic zero

5. Multiply 4 times 23.

6. Place the answer (92) next to the automatic zero.

$$\begin{array}{r} \overset{1}{23} \\ \times\ 45 \\ \hline 115 \\ 920 \end{array}$$ (23 x 5)   (23 x 4)   automatic zero

7. Remember to regroup the 1 above the tens place. The answer is 920. This is the second partial product.

8. Add the two partial products.

9. Remember to place a comma every three digits in the answer starting from the ones place and moving left.

$$\begin{array}{r} 23 \\ \times\ 45 \\ \hline 115 \\ +\ 920 \\ \hline 1,035 \end{array}$$ (23 x 5)   (23 x 40)

10. The answer is 1,035.

Directions: Use the information on page 25 to help you solve these problems. The first two problems are started for you.

1. $\begin{array}{r} 21 \\ \times\ 35 \\ \hline 105 \\ +\ 630 \\ \hline \end{array}$

2. $\begin{array}{r} 43 \\ \times\ 21 \\ \hline 43 \\ +\ 860 \\ \hline \end{array}$

3. $\begin{array}{r} 23 \\ \times\ 41 \\ \hline \end{array}$

4. $\begin{array}{r} 42 \\ \times\ 34 \\ \hline \end{array}$

5. $\begin{array}{r} 54 \\ \times\ 22 \\ \hline \end{array}$

6. $\begin{array}{r} 83 \\ \times\ 33 \\ \hline \end{array}$

7. $\begin{array}{r} 45 \\ \times\ 31 \\ \hline \end{array}$

8. $\begin{array}{r} 51 \\ \times\ 67 \\ \hline \end{array}$

9. $\begin{array}{r} 73 \\ \times\ 53 \\ \hline \end{array}$

10. $\begin{array}{r} 97 \\ \times\ 41 \\ \hline \end{array}$

11. $\begin{array}{r} 65 \\ \times\ 71 \\ \hline \end{array}$

12. $\begin{array}{r} 94 \\ \times\ 62 \\ \hline \end{array}$

13. $\begin{array}{r} 53 \\ \times\ 23 \\ \hline \end{array}$

14. $\begin{array}{r} 87 \\ \times\ 41 \\ \hline \end{array}$

15. $\begin{array}{r} 72 \\ \times\ 14 \\ \hline \end{array}$

16. $\begin{array}{r} 83 \\ \times\ 52 \\ \hline \end{array}$

17. $\begin{array}{r} 82 \\ \times\ 44 \\ \hline \end{array}$

18. $\begin{array}{r} 94 \\ \times\ 82 \\ \hline \end{array}$

19. $\begin{array}{r} 36 \\ \times\ 41 \\ \hline \end{array}$

20. $\begin{array}{r} 79 \\ \times\ 61 \\ \hline \end{array}$

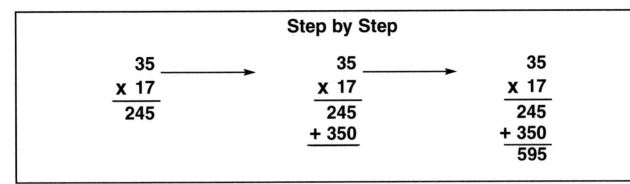

Step by Step

```
   35               35               35
 x 17            x 17             x 17
 ─────           ─────            ─────
  245             245              245
                + 350            + 350
                ─────            ─────
                                  595
```

Directions: Use the information on page 25 and the sample above to help you complete these problems. The first two problems are started for you.

1.   25
   x 64
   ─────
   100
 + 1500

2.   63
   x 34
   ─────
  252
 + 1890

3.   76
   x 41

4.   89
   x 35

5.   76
   x 32

6.   38
   x 43

7.   92
   x 65

8.   36
   x 24

9.   65
   x 24

10.   45
   x 47

11.   44
   x 54

12.   54
   x 83

13.   73
   x 54

14.   59
   x 42

15.   82
   x 27

16.   66
   x 15

17.   65 x 35 = _____

18.   99 x 33 = _____

19.   87 x 23 = _____

20.   43 x 78 = _____

Solving larger multiplication problems is much easier if you remember to go step by step.
1. Use the ladder form to set up your problem.
2. Multiply by the digit in the ones column first.
3. Regroup when necessary.
4. Write the automatic zero.
5. Multiply by the digit in the tens column.
6. Regroup again if necessary.
7. Add the two partial products.
8. Starting from the ones place and moving left, place a comma every three digits.

```
      83
    x 25
     415
     166
   2,075
```

Directions: Use the information on page 25 and the step by step review above to help you complete these problems. The first two problems are started for you.

1.
```
      75
    x 78
     600
  + 5250
```

2.
```
      98
    x 69
     882
  + 5880
```

3.
```
      86
    x 46
```

4.
```
      99
    x 78
```

5.
```
      67
    x 65
```

6.
```
      58
    x 59
```

7.
```
      76
    x 49
```

8.
```
      86
    x 99
```

9. $75 \times 66 =$ _____

10. $77 \times 88 =$ _____

11. $77 \times 55 =$ _____

12. $99 \times 77 =$ _____

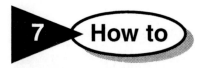

Facts to Know

Commutative Property

The Commutative Property of Multiplication states that when the order of the factors is changed, the product stays the same. Multiplication is a commutative operation. In the equation 2 x 4 = 4 x 2, for example, the order of the factors does not affect the answer (4 x 2 = 8 and 2 x 4 = 8).

The commutative property works for any number of factors. Study the following samples:

Sample A

5 x 6 x 7 = 7 x 6 x 5

5 x 6 x 7 = (210)

7 x 6 x 5 = (210)

Sample B

```
   70              90
 x 90           x 70
(6,300)         (6,300)
```

Sample C

30 x 50 = 50 x 30

30 x 50 = (1,500)

50 x 30 = (1,500)

Associative Property

The Associative Property of Multiplication states that when the grouping of the factors is changed, the product stays the same. Multiplication is associative. The way the factors are grouped with parentheses does not affect the answer. Study the following samples:

Sample D

2 x (3 x 4) = (2 x 3) x 4

2 x (3 x 4) = (24)

(2 x 3) x 4 = (24)

Sample E

6 x (7 x 9) = (6 x 7) x 9

6 x (7 x 9) = (378)

(6 x 7) x 9 = (378)

Sample F

4 x (5 x 6) = (4 x 5) x 6

4 x (5 x 6) = (120)

(4 x 5) x 6 = (120)

Learning these properties will help you better understand multiplication.

Directions: Use the information on page 29 to help you complete the problems below.

1. 5 x 8 = _____

2. 8 x 5 = _____

3. 9 x 6 = _____

4. 6 x 9 = _____

5. 7 x 8 = _____

6. 8 x 7 = _____

7. $\begin{array}{r} 12 \\ \times\ 7 \\ \hline \end{array}$

8. $\begin{array}{r} 7 \\ \times\ 12 \\ \hline \end{array}$

9. $\begin{array}{r} 15 \\ \times\ 8 \\ \hline \end{array}$

10. $\begin{array}{r} 8 \\ \times\ 15 \\ \hline \end{array}$

11. $\begin{array}{r} 18 \\ \times\ 7 \\ \hline \end{array}$

12. $\begin{array}{r} 7 \\ \times\ 18 \\ \hline \end{array}$

13. $\begin{array}{r} 20 \\ \times\ 9 \\ \hline \end{array}$

14. $\begin{array}{r} 9 \\ \times\ 20 \\ \hline \end{array}$

15. $\begin{array}{r} 19 \\ \times\ 6 \\ \hline \end{array}$

16. $\begin{array}{r} 6 \\ \times\ 19 \\ \hline \end{array}$

17. $\begin{array}{r} 17 \\ \times\ 7 \\ \hline \end{array}$

18. $\begin{array}{r} 7 \\ \times\ 17 \\ \hline \end{array}$

Directions: Complete these two-digit times two-digit problems. Remember to regroup where necessary. Check your work. Each pair of answers should be the same.

19. $\begin{array}{r} 90 \\ \times\ 80 \\ \hline \end{array}$

20. $\begin{array}{r} 80 \\ \times\ 90 \\ \hline \end{array}$

21. $\begin{array}{r} 60 \\ \times\ 70 \\ \hline \end{array}$

22. $\begin{array}{r} 70 \\ \times\ 60 \\ \hline \end{array}$

23. $\begin{array}{r} 40 \\ \times\ 90 \\ \hline \end{array}$

24. $\begin{array}{r} 90 \\ \times\ 40 \\ \hline \end{array}$

25. $\begin{array}{r} 80 \\ \times\ 70 \\ \hline \end{array}$

26. $\begin{array}{r} 70 \\ \times\ 80 \\ \hline \end{array}$

27. $\begin{array}{r} 25 \\ \times\ 30 \\ \hline \end{array}$

28. $\begin{array}{r} 30 \\ \times\ 25 \\ \hline \end{array}$

29. $\begin{array}{r} 65 \\ \times\ 40 \\ \hline \end{array}$

30. $\begin{array}{r} 40 \\ \times\ 65 \\ \hline \end{array}$

Study this example.

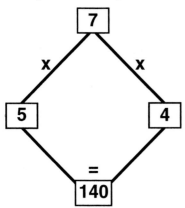 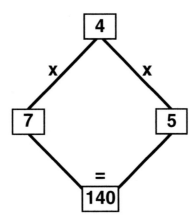 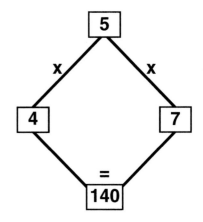

Batter up! Who's on first? Who's on second? Who's on third? It doesn't matter. The score is the same!

4 x 7 x 5 = <u>140</u>   5 x 4 x 7 = <u>140</u>   7 x 5 x 4 = <u>140</u>

Directions: Use the information on page 29 and the example above to help you complete the problems on this page. Check your work. Each set of three problems should have the same answers.

1. 7 x 4 x 8 = _____   5. 8 x 4 x 7 = _____   9. 4 x 7 x 8 = _____

2. 6 x 3 x 4 = _____   6. 4 x 6 x 3 = _____   10. 3 x 6 x 4 = _____

3. 5 x 9 x 3 = _____   7. 3 x 9 x 5 = _____   11. 9 x 3 x 5 = _____

4. 5 x 10 x 9 = _____   8. 9 x 10 x 5 = _____   12. 10 x 5 x 9 = _____

Directions: Complete these problems. Notice which answers are the same.

13. 5 x 6 x 7 x 8 = _____   19. 5 x 9 x 7 x 2 = _____

14. 8 x 7 x 6 x 5 = _____   20. 7 x 9 x 2 x 5 = _____

15. 6 x 5 x 8 x 7 = _____   21. 10 x 11 x 9 x 8 = _____

16. 7 x 8 x 6 x 5 = _____   22. 8 x 10 x 11 x 9 = _____

17. 2 x 5 x 7 x 9 = _____   23. 11 x 10 x 8 x 9 = _____

18. 9 x 7 x 5 x 2 = _____   24. 9 x 10 x 8 x 11 = _____

$3 \times (4 \times 5) = \underline{60}$

$(3 \times 4) \times 5 = \underline{60}$

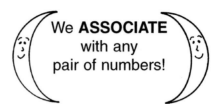

We **ASSOCIATE** with any pair of numbers!

Directions: Use the information on page 29 and the example above to help you complete these problems.

1. $4 \times (5 \times 6) = $ _____

2. $(4 \times 5) \times 6 = $ _____

3. $7 \times (8 \times 9) = $ _____

4. $(7 \times 8) \times 9 = $ _____

5. $(4 \times 6) \times 2 = $ _____

6. $4 \times (6 \times 2) = $ _____

7. $(9 \times 4) \times 7 = $ _____

8. $9 \times (4 \times 7) = $ _____

9. $3 \times (5 \times 9) = $ _____

10. $(3 \times 5) \times 9 = $ _____

Directions: Try these problems. Use the ladder form where needed to do the operation. Review the information on page 17 to multiply by multiples of 10.

11. $(20 \times 30) \times 40 = $ _____

12. $20 \times (30 \times 40) = $ _____

13. $(70 \times 90) \times 30 = $ _____

14. $70 \times (90 \times 30) = $ _____

15. $50 \times (30 \times 80) = $ _____

16. $(50 \times 30) \times 80 = $ _____

17. $(25 \times 40) \times 60 = $ _____

18. $25 \times (40 \times 60) = $ _____

19. $(35 \times 25) \times 10 = $ _____

20. $35 \times (25 \times 10) = $ _____

Facts to Know

To multiply 498 x 76, follow this sample.

Step by Step

1. Write the problem using the ladder form.

   $$\begin{array}{r} 498 \\ \times\ 76 \end{array}$$

2. Multiply 6 ones (6) times 498.

3. Remember to regroup the 4 into the tens place and the 5 into the hundreds place. The answer (6 x 498) is 2,988. This is called a partial product since it represents only part of the product. (**Helpful Hint:** The number of partial products matches the number of digits in the multiplier. For example, if the multiplier is 25 there will be two partial products.)

   $$\begin{array}{r} 54 \\ 498 \\ \times\ 76 \\ \hline 2988 \end{array}$$ partial product (6 x 498)

4. Write the automatic zero in the ones place below the 8. You have already multiplied by the ones place number (6). The zero is a reminder that you are now multiplying by the tens place digit (7).

   $$\begin{array}{r} 54 \\ 498 \\ \times\ 76 \\ \hline 2988 \end{array}$$ (6 x 498)
   0 automatic zero

   cross out or erase →

5. Multiply 7 tens (70) times 498.

   $$\begin{array}{r} \cancel{54} \\ 498 \\ \times\ 76 \end{array}$$

6. Place the answer next to the 0.

   $$\begin{array}{r} 2988 \\ 34860 \end{array}$$ (6 x 498)
   (70 x 498)

7. Remember to regroup the 5 into the tens place and the 6 into the hundreds place.

8. Add the two partial products.

9. Place a comma in the answer every three digits starting at the ones place and moving left.

   $$\begin{array}{r} 498 \\ \times\ 76 \\ \hline 2988 \\ +\ 34860 \\ \hline 37{,}848 \end{array}$$ (6 x 498)
   (70 x 498)

10. The answer is 37,848.

Reminder

- Use the ladder format.
- Regroup when necessary.
- Write the automatic zero.
- Neatly line up the numbers according to place value.
- Add the partial products.
- Starting at the ones place, use commas in the answers every three digits.

Directions: Review the information on page 25 to help you complete these problems. The first two problems are started for you.

1. 88
    x 88
    ────
     704
  + 7040

2. 99
    x 99
    ────
     891
  + 8910

3. 66
    x 66

4. 77
    x 77

5. 69
    x 69

6. 59
    x 59

7. 79
    x 79

8. 89
    x 89

9. 78
    x 78

10. 87
     x 87

11. 49
     x 49

12. 67
     x 67

Directions: Use the information on page 33 to help you complete the problems on this page. The first two problems are started for you. (Remember to use automatic zeros, to regroup where necessary, and to add the partial products.)

1.   308
     x   45
     1540
   + 12320

2.   709
     x   95
     3545
   + 63810

3.   506
     x   64

4.   109
     x   29

5.   705
     x   67

6.   509
     x   56

7.   909
     x   37

8.   806
     x   28

9.   803
     x   76

10.   906
      x   49

11.   409
      x   88

12.   807
      x   39

13.   111
      x   33

14.   222
      x   11

15.   555
      x   22

16.   333
      x   44

When you multiply larger numbers, such as two-, three-, and four-digit multipliers and multiplicands, there are many steps to complete before you arrive at a product. Forgotten automatic zeros, for example, can result in an answer that is 100, even 1000 higher or lower than the exact product. You can check to see whether your answer is at least close to the actual product by estimating the product.

Round to estimate the product. (**Reminder:** For numbers 5 through 9, round up. For numbers 1 through 4, round down.)

76	Round 76 to 80	80		825	Round 825 to 800	800
X 21	Round 21 to 20	X 20		X 298	Round 298 to 300	X 300
1,596		1,600		245,850		240,000
Actual Product		**Estimated Product**		**Actual Product**		**Estimated Product**

Directions: Use the information above and on page 17 (multiplying with multiples of 10) to help you complete the problems below. Estimate the products. Then, solve the problem and compare the actual product to the estimated product. The first problem has been done for you.

Actual Product	Estimated Product		Actual Product	Estimated Product
1. 93	90	**2.**	17	
x 27	x 30		x 87	
651	2,700			
1860				
2,511				

3. 75		**4.**	88	
x 24			x 12	

5. 53		**6.**	235	
x 82			x 605	

7. 778		**8.**	904	
x 385			x 558	

Facts to Know

Common Factors

- A *factor* is a number which divides evenly into another number. The number 6 divides evenly into 12. It is a factor of 12.

- When two numbers are multiplied, they are factors of the answer.

  In the equation 2 x 6 = 12, the numbers 2 and 6 are factors of 12.

  The number 1 is always a factor of every number.

- A *common factor* is a number which is a factor of two different products.

  Since the number 6 is a factor of 12 and a factor of 18, it is a common factor of both numbers.

  ### Sample A

  The factors of 12 are 1, 2, 3, 4, 6, and 12.

  The factors of 18 are 1, 2, 3, 6, 9, and 18.

  The common factors are 1, 2, 3, and 6.

Common Multiples

- A *multiple* is the number made when any two factors are multiplied together. It is the product of two factors.

  In the equation 2 x 6 = 12, the number 12 is a multiple of 2 and 6.

- A *common multiple* is a number that is a product of the same factor as another number.

  The number 12 is a common multiple of both 2 and 3.

  The number 6 is a common multiple of both 2 and 3.

  The number 18 is a common multiple of both 2 and 3.

- Some common multiples of 2 and 3 are 6, 12, and 18.

  ### Sample B

  The multiples of 2 are 2, 4, 6, 8, 10, 12, 14, 16, 18, and 20.

  The multiples of 3 are 3, 6, 9, 12, 15, and 18.

Simple Exponents

- When a number is to be multiplied by itself, it can be written as an exponent.

- An *exponent* tells how many times to multiply the base number by itself.

  The number 4 written as an exponent of the base number 3 (3^4) means multiply 3 four times or 3 x 3 x 3 x 3 (81).

  ### Sample C

  $3^4 = 3 \times 3 \times 3 \times 3 = 81$

Common factors are numbers that are factors of two different products. The factors 1,2,3, and 6 are common to 12 and 18.

(①, 12, ②, ⑥, ③, 4)   (①, 18, ②, 9, ③, ⑥)

Factors of 12   **Factors of 18**

Directions: Circle the common factors for each pair of numbers.

1.   8 (1, 2, 4, 8)   **5.**   10 (1, 2, 5, 10)
     12 (1, 2, 3, 4, 6, 12)   20 (1, 2, 4, 5, 10, 20)

2.   6 (1, 2, 3, 6)   **6.**   12 (1, 2, 3, 4, 6, 12)
     8 (1, 2, 4, 8)   24 (1, 2, 3, 4, 6, 8, 12, 24)

3.   10 (1, 2, 5, 10)   **7.**   8 (1, 2, 4, 8)
     15 (1, 3, 5, 15)   10 (1, 2, 5, 10)

4.   16 (1, 2, 4, 8, 16)   **8.**   24 (1, 2, 3, 4, 6, 8, 12, 24)
     24 (1, 2, 3, 4, 6, 8, 12, 24)   28 (1, 2, 4, 7, 14, 28)

Directions: List the factors for each number in the problems below. Circle the common factors.

9.   6 (1, 2, 3, 6)   **14.**   24
     10 (___ , ___ , ___ , ___)   30

10.   9 (___ , ___ , ___)   **15.**   32
     18 (___ , ___ , ___ , ___ , ___ , ___)   16

11.   12   **16.**   48
     16   36

12.   7   **17.**   36
     14   18

13.   10   **18.**   18
     30   12

Directions: List the factors for each number. Circle the common factors for each set of three numbers.

19.   6 (1, 2, 3, 6)   **21.**   10
     12 (___ , ___ , ___ , ___ , ___ , ___)   15
     18 (___ , ___ , ___ , ___ , ___ , ___)   25

20.   9   **22.**   16
     12   24
     24   36

A *multiple* is the product of two factors.

A *common multiple* is a number that is a product of the same factor as another number.

To find the multiples of a number, multiply that number by 1, then 2, then 3, etc.

Here are the first six multiples of 4 and 6.

4 (4, 8, 12, 16, 20, 24)
6 (6, 12, 18, 24, 30, 36)

The numbers 12 and 24 are common multiples of both 4 and 6.

Directions: Find and circle the common multiples of the pairs of factors named below.

1. 3 (3, 6, 9, 12, 15, 18)
    2 (2, 4, 6, 8, 10, 12, 14, 16, 18)

4. 6 (6, 12, 18, 24)
    8 (8, 16, 24)

2. 4 (4, 8, 12, 16, 20, 24)
    2 (2, 4, 6, 8, 10, 12, 14, 16, 18, 20, 22, 24)

5. 9 (9, 18, 27, 36)
    6 (6, 12, 18, 24, 36)

3. 9 (9, 18, 27, 36)
    4 (4, 8, 12, 16, 20, 24, 28, 32, 36)

6. 12 (12, 24, 36)
    9 (9, 18, 27, 36)

Directions: List the first six multiples for each of the sets of numbers named below. Circle the common multiples.

7. 9 (9, 18, 27, 36, 45, 54)

    3 (___ , ___ , ___ , ___ , ___ , ___)

9. 10 (___ , ___ , ___ , ___ , ___ , ___)

    5 (___ , ___ , ___ , ___ , ___ , ___)

8. 12 (___ ___ , ___ , ___ , ___ , ___)

    10 (___ , ___ , ___ , ___ , ___ , ___)

10. 3 (___ , ___ , ___ , ___ , ___ , ___)

    12 (___ , ___ , ___ , ___ , ___ , ___)

A number multiplied by itself can be written as an exponent. The exponent tells how many times to multiply the base number by itself.

3^2 **means multiply 3 by itself two times** $3^2 = 3 \times 3 = 9$
5^2 **means multiply 5 by itself five times** $5^2 = 5 \times 5 = 9$

The number 3^2 can be read "three to the second power" or "three squared."

Directions: For each of the terms below, write an equation and solve it. The first two problems are done for you.

1. 4^2 $4 \times 4 = 16$
2. 5^2 $5 \times 5 = 25$
3. 2^2 _____ x _____ = _____
4. 3^2 _____ x _____ = _____
5. 6^2

6. 8^2
7. 10^2
8. 9^2
9. 7^2
10. 12^2

Directions: For each of the terms below, write two equations and solve them. The first two are done for you.

11. 2^3 $2 \times 2 = 4$
         $4 \times 2 = 8$
      2^3 $= 8$

12. 3^3 $3 \times 3 = 9$
         $9 \times 3 = 27$
      3^3 $= 27$

13. 4^3 _____ x _____ = _____
         _____ x _____ = _____
      4^3 = _____

14. 6^3 _____ x _____ = _____
         _____ x _____ = _____
      6^3 = _____

15. 7^3 _____ x _____ = _____
         _____ x _____ = _____
      7^3 = _____

16. 9^3 _____ x _____ = _____
         _____ x _____ = _____
      9^3 = _____

17. 5^3 _____ x _____ = _____
         _____ x _____ = _____
      5^3 = _____

18. 8^3 _____ x _____ = _____
         _____ x _____ = _____
      8^3 = _____

19. 10^3 _____ x _____ = _____
         _____ x _____ = _____
      10^3 = _____

20. 12^3 _____ x _____ = _____
         _____ x _____ = _____
      12^3 = _____

Directions: Read each animal problem. Use what you have learned in this book to solve the problems.

Lizard Lore

1. A green anole is 8 inches long. If you lined up 4 green anoles from nose to tail, how long would the line be?_____

2. A western fence lizard is 7 inches long. How long a line would 9 fence lizards make?_____

3. A western fence lizard can lay 9 eggs. How many eggs would 8 fence lizards lay?_____

4. A common tree lizard lays 9 eggs in one clutch (group). She may lay 6 clutches a year. How many eggs could she lay in one year?_____

5. The jungle runner can be 25 inches long. How long could a line of 8 jungle runners reach?_____

6. A five-lined skink lays 15 eggs. How many eggs would 9 skinks lay?_____

7. The western skink is 23 centimeters long. How long would a line of 5 of these skinks be?_____

8. A ground skink is 13 centimeters long. A Racer snake is 8 times as long. How many centimeters long is the Racer?_____

9. A Desert Iguana is 25 centimeters long. The Common Iguana is 8 times as long. How many centimeters long is the Common Iguana?_____

10. The bunch grass lizard lays 12 eggs in a clutch (group). How many eggs would 9 bunch grass lizards lay?_____

Tree Tales

1. A pussy willow is 20 feet high. A Giant Sequoia is 10 times as tall. How tall is the Sequoia?_____

2. A cone of a white pine is 15 centimeters long. The tree stands 100 times as high as the cone. How many centimeters high is the tree?_____

3. A cone of a California juniper is 12 millimeters long. The tree is 1,000 times as tall. How many millimeters tall is the tree?_____

4. The fruit of a sweet cherry is 2 centimeters across. The tree is 1,000 times as tall. How many centimeters tall is the tree?_____

5. The cone of a giant sequoia is 6 centimeters long. The width of the tree is 100 times as much. How many centimeters wide is the tree?_____

6. The trunk of a California black oak is 90 centimeters across. The tree's height is 10 times as much. How many centimeters tall is the tree?_____

7. A leaf of the white mulberry is 12 centimeters long. The tree is 100 times as tall. How many centimeters tall is the tree?_____

8. A leaf of a Texas mulberry is 2 centimeters wide. The trunk of the tree is 10 times as wide. How many centimeters wide is the trunk of the tree?_____

9. A leaf from an apple tree is 9 centimeters long. The tree is 100 times as tall. How tall is the tree?_____

10. A leaf from a California sycamore is 23 centimeters long. The tree is 100 times as tall. How tall is the tree?_____

Directions: Read each insect and calculator problem. Use what you have learned in this book to solve the problems.

Buggy Facts

1. A queen termite lays 25 eggs a minute. How many eggs can she lay in 60 minutes?_____

2. A swallowtail butterfly beats it wings 300 times in one minute. How many times will the wings beat in 60 minutes?_____

3. The world's largest grasshopper is 25 centimeters long. It can jump 19 times its length. How many centimeters can it jump?_____

4. There are about 20 new species of insects discovered every day. How many species of insects are discovered in a year?_____

5. A cricket is 25 millimeters long. It can jump 30 times its own length. How far can it jump?_____

6. A female silkworm can lay 700 eggs. How many eggs could 30 silkworms lay?_____

7. A monarch butterfly can travel 80 miles a day when it migrates. How far can it travel in 23 days?_____

8. A ladybug may lay 500 eggs in her lifetime. How many eggs would 25 ladybugs lay?_____

9. A ladybug may eat 250 aphids a day. How many aphids could it eat in 21 days?_____

10. One kind of ladybug has 13 spots on its back. How many spots would 32 of these ladybugs have?_____

Body Stuff

Use this information to solve the following problems on your calculator.

1 minute = 60 seconds   **1 day = 24 hours**
1 hour = 60 minutes   **1 year = 365 days**

1. A child's heart beats about 90 times a minute.

   How many times does it beat in 1 hour?_____

   How many times does it beat in 1 day?_____

2. The heart pumps about 4 quarts of blood each minute.

   How many quarts of blood does it pump in 1 day?_____

   How many quarts of blood does it pump in 1 year?_____

3. Your mouth makes about 48 ounces of saliva in one day.

   How much saliva does it make in 1 year?_____

   How much saliva does it make in 70 years?_____

4. The average person has about 100,000 hairs on his or her head.

   How many hairs would a class of 35 students have?_____

   How many hairs would a school with 500 students have?_____

5. An adult has about 206 bones in his or her body.

   How many bones would a group of 25 teachers have?_____

6. A child has about 144 ounces of blood.

   How many ounces of blood would a class of 30 children have?_____

1 minute = 60 seconds	**1 day = 24 hours**
1 hour = 60 minutes	**1 year = 365 days**

Directions: Use the information above and what you have learned about multiplication in this book to solve these problems.

1. Brushing your teeth with the water running uses about 5 gallons of water.
   - How much water would you use to brush your teeth 3 times in one day?_____
   - How much water would you use to brush your teeth 3 times in one year?
     _____

2. For a family of 4 people, washing dishes with the faucet on will use 30 gallons of water each day.
   - How much water would be used to wash dishes in 1 year?_____
   - How much water would a street with 20 houses use in 1 year to wash the dishes?_____

3. For the same size family, it takes only 5 gallons a day to wash dishes in the sink with the water off.
   - How much water would be used to wash dishes in 1 year?_____
   - How much water would a street with 20 houses use in 1 year to wash the dishes this way?_____

4. It takes only 10 gallons of water to wash a car at a self-service car wash.
   - How much water would it take to wash a car every week for a year?_____
     It can take 15 times as much water to wash a car with the hose running at home.
   - How much water would be used in 1 year to wash a car at home?_____

5. If your father shaves with the water on, it can take 20 gallons of water each time he shaves.
   - How much water would he use to shave once a day for a year?_____
     If he fills the basin with water, it only takes 1 gallon.
   - How much water would he use to shave once a day for a year?_____

1 week = 7 days   **1 day = 24 hours**

1 year = 365 days

Directions: Use the information above and what you have learned about multiplication in this book to solve these problems.

1. A five minute shower uses 35 gallons of water.

   • If you take 1 shower a day, how many gallons of water would you use in a year?_____

   • If your family takes a total of 6 showers a day, how much water would they use every day?_____

   • If your family takes 6 showers a day, how much water would they use every year?_____

2. Low-flow shower heads use only 15 gallons of water for a five-minute shower.

   • If you take 1 low-flow shower a day, how many gallons of water would you use in a year?_____

   • If your family takes a total of 6 low-flow showers a day, how much water would they use every day?_____

   • If your family takes 6 low-flow showers a day, how much water would they use a year?_____

3. The average toilet is flushed 8 times a day. Each flush uses about 1½ gallons of water.

   • How much water would be used every day in a house with 2 toilets?_____

   • How much water would be used every week in a house with 2 toilets?_____

   • How much water would be used every year in a house with 2 toilets?_____

4. It takes about 40 gallons of water to wash a load of clothes.

   • How much water would be used to wash 3 loads of clothes every day for a week?_____

   • How much water would be used to wash 3 loads of clothes every day for a year?_____

•••••••• **Computing Multiplication Facts**

Before You Begin

For this activity, you will create a formula on the computer that will calculate multiplication facts. You will need access to a computer and a spreadsheet program such as *Microsoft Excel®* or AppleWorks® (*ClarisWorks®*). If you have not used a spreadsheet, read the following information and have someone familiar with spreadsheet programs help you start this activity. It is important to understand the basics of a spreadsheet such as a cell, the name of each cell (A1 or C8 for example), and how to enter data into the cells on a spreadsheet.

Spreadsheet software is computer software that allows the user to enter numbers and formulas into a grid or chart style format. Formulas automatically perform the calculation on the entered numbers. This provides the user with answers quickly and accurately. Many spreadsheet programs also have a graphing function that works with a spreadsheet to create graphic representations of data.

Instructions

1. Create your multiplication table by first launching a spreadsheet.

2. Begin in cell A2 and enter the numbers 1–2 going down. (See page 46.)

3. Enter the number 1 in cell B1. (See page 46.) This number represents the other factor. In other words, you will be multiplying the factor 1 times each factor in the cells of column A.

4. Click on B2. You are directing the computer to multiply cell A2 by cell B1 (2 x 1). You will notice that a spreadsheet formula always starts with the equal sign, so in cell B2, the formula would be =B1*A2.

5. Press Enter or Return after placing the formula in the cell. Notice that when you press Enter or Return, the answer of the multiplication facts goes into the cell.

6. Click on B3 and enter the following formula: =B1*A3. Continue this process of entering formulas until you have completed the cell entries in column B. (See page 46.)

You are now ready to compute multiplication facts for factors other than 1. Simply click on cell B1 and change the number to 4, 7, 9, or another factor and watch what happens! Once you press enter, all the other numbers in the column compute to show the products. Change the number in cell B1 to 45 or 92 and watch the computer calculate the products.

Spreadsheet Sample for Computing Multiplication Facts

Use these spreadsheet samples with the instructions on page 45.

Steps 1 and 2
Enter numbers.

	A	B	C
1		1	
2	1		
3	2		
4	3		
5	4		
6	5		
7	6		
8	7		
9	8		
10	9		
11	10		
12	11		
13	12		
14			
15			

Steps 3-6
Enter formulas.

	A	B	C
1		1	
2	1	=B1*A2	
3	2	=B1*A3	
4	3	=B1*A4	
5	4	=B1*A5	
6	5	=B1*A6	
7	6	=B1*A7	
8	7	=B1*A8	
9	8	=B1*A9	
10	9	=B1*A10	
11	10	=B1*A11	
12	11	=B1*A12	
13	12	=B1*A13	
14			
15			

Reminder: After the formula is entered, press Enter or Return. The formula will change to the product (answer) of the two factors that are being multiplied. Once all formulas are entered, change the number in B1 to a higher number and watch all the answers change.

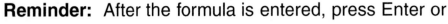

Page 6
1. 32
2. 32
3. 30
4. 30
5. 21
6. 21
7. 45
8. 45
9. 72
10. 72
11. 40
12. 40
13. 42
14. 32
15. 63
16. 72
17. 96
18. 35
19. 64
20. 72
21. 24
22. 121
23. 56
24. 63

Page 7
sample 24
1. 54
2. 49
3. 40
4. 36
5. 72
6. 64
7. 56
8. 54
9. 55
10. 24
11. 36
12. 96
13. 99
14. 56
15. 24
16. 12
17. 12
18. 108
19. 108
20. 110
21. 110
22. 35
23. 35
24. 48
25. 48
26. 63
27. 63
28. 49
29. 81
30. 144
31. 36
32. 25
33. 100

Page 8
sample 18, 20, 22, 24
1. 21, 24, 27, 30
2. 30, 35, 40, 45, 50, 55, 60
3. 20, 24, 28, 32, 36, 40, 44, 48
4. 45, 54, 63, 72, 81, 90, 99, 108
5. 50, 60, 70, 80, 90, 100, 110, 120
6. 35, 42, 49, 56, 63, 70, 77, 84
7. 10, 12, 14, 16, 18, 20, 22, 24
8. 5, 6, 7, 8, 9, 10, 11, 12
9. 30, 36, 42, 48, 54, 60, 66, 72
10. 72, 84, 96, 108, 120, 132, 144
11. 3
12. 12
14. 78
15. 10

Page 10
1. 21
2. 20
3. 42
4. 27
5. 40
6. 48
7. 45
8. 36
9. 24
10. 36
11. 42
12. 54
13. 99
14. 96
15. 80
16. 40
17. 9
18. 81
19. 48
20. 72
21. 33
22. 99
23. 49
24. 63
25. 88
26. 77
27. 18
28. 66
29. 33
30. 90

Page 11
1. 5, 2, 3
2. 7, 2, 2
3. 7, 2, 3
4. 11, 2, 2
5. 5, 2, 5
6. 11, 2, 3
7. 11, 7
8. 7, 3, 3
9. 3, 5
10. 2, 3, 3
11. 11, 2
12. 2, 2, 3, 3
13. 2, 2, 2
14. 2, 2, 2, 2, 2
15. 5, 5
16. 5, 5, 5

Page 12
1. 8
2. 8
3. 9
4. 5
5. 6
6. 5
7. 3
8. 9
9. 9
10. 7
11. 9
12. 12
13. 8
14. 9
15. 9
16. 8
17. 8
18. 4
19. 9
20. 5
21. 11
22. 11
23. 2
24. 5
25. 8, 8
26. 10,1 0
27. 6, 6
28. 9, 9
29. 7, 7
30. 11, 11

Page 14
1. 128
2. 129
3. 28
4. 99
5. 46
6. 48
7. 86
8. 67
9. 68
10. 146
11. 124
12. 69
13. 205
14. 88
15. 88
16. 186
17. 48
18. 99

Page 15
1. 117
2. 441
3. 154
4. 148
5. 288
6. 330
7. 175
8. 228
9. 378
10. 108
11. 235
12. 440
13. 252
14. 325
15. 756
16. 525
17. 486
18. 891
19. 343
20. 632

Page 16
1. 1,107
2. 2,568
3. 615
4. 2,595
5. 3,708
6. 6,223
7. 3,320
8. 6,237
9. 4,434
10. 5,229
11. 8,991
12. 2,752
13. 5,495
14. 1,821
15. 6,279
16. 4,216
17. 3,944
18. 981

Page 18
1. 140
2. 160
3. 450
4. 650
5. 190
6. 170
7. 220
8. 370
9. 380
10. 980
11. 760
12. 650
13. 680
14. 770
15. 730
16. 330
17. 350
18. 530
19. 9,860
20. 8,720
21. 6,210
22. 7,650
23. 5,430
24. 97,670
25. 75,020
26. 10,430
27. 89,760
28. 60,040

Page 19
1. 700
2. 800
3. 400
4. 4,300
5. 3,200
6. 5,100
7. 5,400
8. 2,600
9. 6,200
10. 9,800
11. 98,900
12. 44,700
13. 82,600
14. 7,300
15. 65,900
16. 74,900
17. 897,400
18. 543,900
19. 563,800
20. 654,900
21. 873,200
22. 2,220,200
23. 6,580,400
24. 9,752,700
25. 76,590,500

Page 20
1. 5,000
2. 7,000
3. 3,000
4. 65,000
5. 23,000
6. 14,000
7. 67,00
8. 21,000
9. 99,000
10. 76,000
11. 654,000
12. 785,000
13. 806,000
14. 117,000
15. 3,943,000
16. 4,607,000
17. 1,840,000
18. 5,006,000
19. 9,478,000
20. 2,001,000
21. 7,958,000
22. 2,980,000
23. 43,767,000
24. 99,759,000
25. 876,423,000
26. 756,000,000

Page 22
1. 360
2. 280
3. 390
4. 760
5. 360
6. 800
7. 1,080
8. 630
9. 560
10. 2,430
11. 1,080
12. 1,250
13. 570
14. 1,540
15. 8,010
16. 2,310
17. 3,960
18. 5,850
19. 340
20. 3,690
21. 1,140
22. 940
23. 1,720
24. 6,960
25. 1,340
26. 2,340

Page 23
1. 12,000
2. 45,000
3. 54,000
4. 28,000
5. 64,000
6. 35,000
7. 14,000
8. 24,000
9. 42,000
10. 9,000
11. 21,000
12. 42,000
13. 6,080
14. 72,560
15. 63,140
16. 20,360
17. 10,450
18. 28,360
19. 36,180
20. 24,270
21. 4,420
22. 18,960
23. 51,870
24. 15,450
25. 26,190
26. 32,920
27. 18,880
28. 51,780

Page 24
1. 46,400
2. 115,200
3. 366,500
4. 269,200
5. 166,600
6. 262,800
7. 289,800
8. 360,500
9. 184,400
10. 196,800
11. 469,800
12. 613,900
13. 255,200
14. 286,200
15. 219,600
16. 93,000
17. 152,600
18. 193,200
19. 478,000
20. 102,300
21. 316,000
22. 467,000
23. 166,500
24. 117,000
25. 557,400

Page 26
1. 735
2. 903
3. 943
4. 1,428
5. 1,188
6. 2,739
7. 1,395
8. 3,417
9. 3,869
10. 3,977
11. 4,615
12. 5,828
13. 1,219
14. 3,567
15. 1,008
16. 4,316
17. 3,608
18. 7,708
19. 1,476
20. 4,819

Page 27
1. 1,600
2. 2,142
3. 3,116
4. 3,115
5. 2,432
6. 1,634
7. 5,980
8. 864
9. 1,560
10. 2,115
11. 2,376
12. 4,482
13. 3,942
14. 2,478
15. 2,214
16. 990
17. 2,275
18. 3,267
19. 2,001
20. 3,354

Page 28
1. 5,850
2. 6,762
3. 3,956
4. 7,722
5. 4,355
6. 3,422
7. 3,724
8. 8,514
9. 4,950
10. 6,776
11. 4,235
12. 7,623

Page 30
1. 40
2. 40
3. 54
4. 54
5. 56
6. 56

7. 84
8. 84
9. 120
10. 120
11. 126
12. 126
13. 180
14. 180
15. 114
16. 114
17. 119
18. 119
19. 7,200
20. 7,200
21. 4,200
22. 4,200
23. 3,600
24. 3,600
25. 5,600
26. 5,600
27. 750
28. 750
29. 2,600
30. 2,600

Page 31
1. 224
2. 224
3. 224
4. 72
5. 72
6. 72
7. 135
8. 135
9. 135
10. 450
11. 450
12. 450
13. 1,680
14. 1,680
15. 1,680
16. 1,680
17. 630
18. 630
19. 630
20. 630
21. 7,920
22. 7,920
23. 7,920
24. 7,920

Page 32
1. 120
2. 120
3. 504
4. 504
5. 48
6. 48
7. 252
8. 252
9. 135
10. 135
11. 24,000
12. 24,000

13. 189,000
14. 189,000
15. 120,000
16. 120,000
17. 60,000
18. 60,000
19. 8,750
20. 8,750

Page 34
1. 7,744
2. 9,801
3. 4,356
4. 5,929
5. 4,761
6. 3,481
7. 6,241
8. 7,921
9. 6,084
10. 7,569
11. 2,401
12. 4,489

Page 35
1. 13,860
2. 67,355
3. 32,384
4. 3,161
5. 47,235
6. 28,504
7. 33,633
8. 22,568
9. 61,028
10. 44,394
11. 35,992
12. 31,473
13. 3,663
14. 2,442
15. 12,210
16. 14,652

Page 36
Actual Products
1. 2,511
2. 1,479
3. 1,800
4. 1,056
5. 4,346
6. 142,175
7. 299,530
8. 504,432

Page 38
1. 1, 2, 4
2. 1, 2
3. 1, 5
4. 1, 2, 4, 8
5. 1, 2, 5, 10
6. 1, 2, 3, 4, 6, 12
7. 1, 2
8. 1, 2, 4
9. 6: 1, 2, 3, 6 10: 1, 2, 5, 10
   CF: 1, 2
10. 9: 1, 3, 9 18: 1, 2, 3, 6, 9, 18
    CF: 1, 3, 9
11. 12: 1, 2, 3, 4, 6, 12 16: 1, 2,
    4, 8, 16 CF: 1, 2, 4
12. 7: 1, 7 14: 1, 2, 7, 14 CF: 1, 7
13. 10: 1, 2, 5, 10 30: 1, 2, 3, 5,
    6, 15, 30 CF: 1, 2, 5
14. 24: 1, 2, 3, 4, 6, 12, 24 30: 1,
    2, 3, 5, 6, 15, 30 CF: 1, 2, 3, 6
15. 32: 1, 2, 4, 8, 16, 32 16: 1, 2,
    4, 8, 16 CF: 1, 2, 4, 8, 16
16. 48: 1, 2, 3, 4, 6, 8, 12, 18, 24,
    48 36: 1, 2, 3, 4, 6, 9, 12, 18,
    36 CF: 1, 2, 3, 4, 6, 12, 18
17. 36: 1, 2, 3, 4, 6, 9, 12, 18, 36
    18: 1, 2, 3, 6, 9, 18 CF: 1, 2,
    3, 6, 9, 18
18. 18: 1, 2, 3, 6, 9, 18 12: 1, 2,
    3, 4, 6, 12, 18 CF: 1, 2, 3, 6
19. 6: 1, 2, 3, 6 12: 1, 2, 3, 4, 6, 12
    18: 1, 2, 3, 6, 9, 18 C.F. 1, 2,
    3, 6
20. 9: 1, 3, 9 12: 1, 2, 3, 4, 6, 12
    24: 1, 2, 3, 4, 6, 8, 12, 24 1, 3
21. 10: 1, 2, 5, 10 15: 1, 3, 5, 15
    25: 1, 5, 25 C.F. 1, 5
22. 16: 1, 2, 4, 8, 16
    24: 1, 2, 3, 4, 6, 8, 12, 24
    36: 1, 2, 3, 4, 6, 9, 12, 18, 36
    C.F. 1, 2, 4

Page 39
1. 3: 3, 6, 9, 12, 15, 18/2: 2, 34,
   6, 8, 10, 12, 14, 16, 18, 20,
   22, 24 CM: 6, 12, 18
2. 4: 4, 8, 12,16, 20, 24/2: 2, 4,
   6, 8, 10, 12, 14, 16, 18, 20, 22,
   24 CM: 4, 8, 12, 16, 20, 24
3. 6: 6, 12, 18, 24/8: 8, 16, 24
   CM: 24
4. 9: 9, 18, 27, 36 6: 6, 12, 18,
   24, 36 CM: 18, 36
5. 9: 9, 18, 27, 36/4: 4, 8, 12,16,
   20, 24 CM: 36
6. 12: 12, 24, 36/9: 9, 18, 27, 36
   CM: 36
7. 9:9, 18, 27, 36, 45, 54
   3: 3, 6, 9, 12, 15, 18 CM: 9
8. 12: 12, 24, 36, 48, 60, 72
   10: 10, 20, 30, 40, 50, 60
   CM: 60
9. 10: 10, 20, 30, 40, 50, 60
   5: 5, 10, 15, 20, 25, 30
   CM: 30
10. 3: 3, 6, 9, 12, 15, 18/12: 12,
    24, 36, 48, 60, 72 CM: 12

Page 40
1. 16
2. 25
3. 2, 2, 4
4. 3, 3, 9
5. 6, 6, 36
6. 8, 8, 64
7. 10, 10, 100
8. 9, 9, 81
9. 7, 7, 49
10. 12, 12, 144
11. 4, 8, 8
12. 9, 27, 27
13. 4, 4, 16/
    16, 4, 64/64
14. 6, 6, 36
    36, 6, 216/216

15. 7, 7, 49/ 49,
    7, 343/343
16. 9, 9, 81/ 81,
    9, 729/ 729
17. 5, 5, 25/25,
    5, 125/125
18. 8, 8, 64/64,
    8, 512/512
19. 10, 10, 100/
    100, 10,
    1,000/ 1,000
20. 12, 12, 144/
    144, 12,
    1,728/1,728

Page 41

Lizard Lore
1. 32 inches
2. 63 inches
3. 72 eggs
4. 54 eggs
5. 200 inches
6. 135 eggs
7. 115 cm
8. 104 cm
9. 200 cm
10. 108 eggs

Tree Tales
1. 200 feet
2. 1,500 cm
3. 12,000 mm
4. 2,000 cm
5. 600 cm
6. 900 cm
7. 1,200 cm
8. 20 cm
9. 900 cm
10. 2,300 cm

Page 42
Buggy Facts
1. 1,500 eggs
2. 18,000 times
3. 475 cm
4. 7,300 species
5. 750 mm
6. 21,000 eggs
7. 1,840 miles
8. 12,500 eggs
9. 5,250 aphids
10. 416 spots

Body Stuff
1. 5,400 times / 129,600 times
2. 5,760 quarts / 87,600 quarts
3. 17,520 ounces / 1,226,400 ounces
4. 3,500,000 hairs / 50,000,000 hairs
5. 5,150 bones
6. 4,320 ounces

Page 43
1. 15 gallons / 5,475 gallons
2. 10,950 gallons / 219,000 gallons
3. 1,825 gallons / 36,500 gallons
4. 520 gallons / 7,800 gallons
5. 7,300 gallons / 365 gallons

Page 44
1. 12,775 gallons / 210 gallons /
   76,650 gallons
2. 5,475 gallons / 90 gallons /
   32,850 gallons
3. 24 gallons / 168 gallons / 8,760
   gallons
4. 840 gallons / 43,800 gallons